Calm the Fuck Down

A Humorous And Inappropriate Adult Coloring Book

Oancea Camelia

Piss of

i am sick
of
this
shit

CALM
THE
FUCK
DOWN

Something
to do until
the Valium
kicks in

LET
THAT
SHIT
GO

ASSHOLE

Seriously
Bitch?

damn it

SUCK IT UP,
BUTTERCUP

best
fucking
friends

bitch

bullshit

Namaste. Now fuck off.

MEH

BASTARD

PRICK

whore

MOTHERFUCKER

FUCKWIT

FUCK
FACE

COLORING
MOTHERFUCKER

FUCK
THIS
SHIT

clusterfuck

BULLSHIT

bloody
bitch

MORON

FUCKING
MAGICAL

TODAY IS GOING TO BE FUCKED UP

my
middlefinger
likes you

NO
NO
NO

FUCK OFF

CALM THE FUCK DOWN

CHILL
THE
FUCK
OUT

SIT THE
FUCK DOWN
AND COLOR

FUCK
MY LIFE

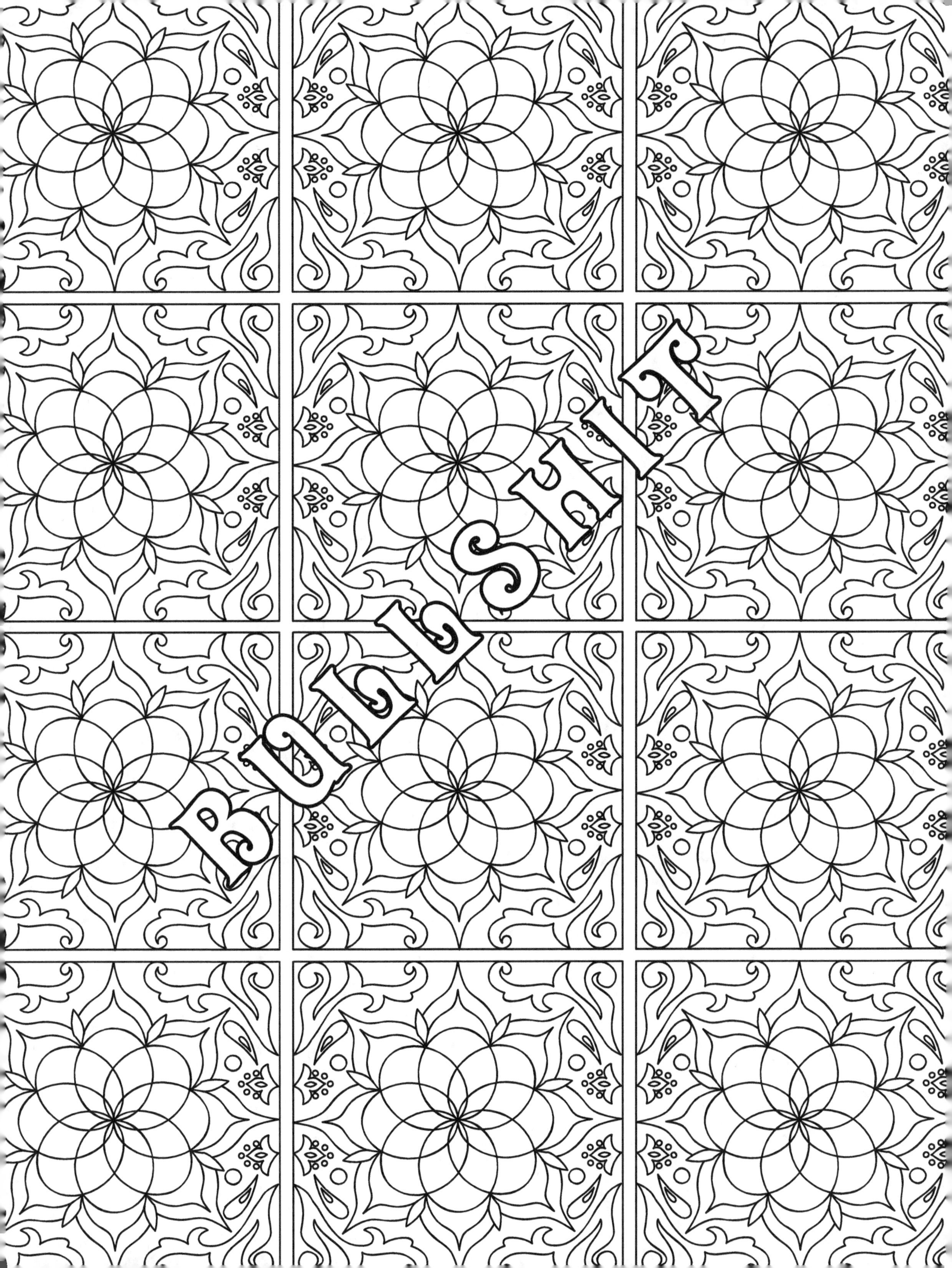
BULLSHIT

KISS MY SHINY ASS

CRAP

FUCK
FUCK

what the fuck is this?

www.ingramcontent.com/pod-product-compliance
Lightning Source LLC
Chambersburg PA
CBHW081236280526
45787CB00006B/2674
* 9 7 8 1 5 3 2 9 6 3 7 5 9 *